TINY PANTONE® OBJECTS

PANTONE®
2726 C

PANTONE®
200 C

PANTONE®
621 C

PANTONE®
143 C

PANTONE®
728 C

TINY PANTONE OBJECTS

INKA MATHEW

ABRAMS IMAGE, NEW YORK

INTRODUCTION

Have you ever seen a flower and then wondered if you could find a PANTONE® color match for it? Maybe not, but that's exactly the question that started the "Tiny PMS® Match" project. What began with my curiosity has become a personal, significant project of tiny proportion, in which I match everyday little objects to their corresponding PANTONE MATCHING SYSTEM® (PMS) colors. I color-match objects that pique my interest and also those that have special meaning to me. This project is also my visual journal: It has allowed me to capture the little things in my life—literally— such as my son's Lego toys, my daughter's Minion Tic Tacs, and my favorite Disney character, Totoro.

As a print graphic designer, I am surrounded by colors. PANTONE solid color chips are my tools of trade. I get a unique satisfaction from matching little objects around me to their exact PANTONE colors. Maybe, by doing it, I create some small sense of order in the world around me. I found out that this desire for order is something that I share with a lot of people around the world.

My "Tiny PMS Match" Tumblr blog has garnered tens of thousands of followers, and many of them have told me that looking at the color-matched photos made them feel happy, calm, and relaxed. Hearing that only added more joy to my color-matching hobby.

Tiny PANTONE® Objects is a book that was born out of my "Tiny PMS Match" project. I am delighted to have the opportunity for these images to be collected and turned into a book. My hope is that as you flip through its pages, this book will give you calm in the middle of your busy day. And I hope these colorful, playful images will bring out the child in you.

—Inka Mathew

PANTONE®
Yellow C

6 PANTONE Yellow C color match
Plastic Pikachu head

PANTONE®
101 C

PANTONE 101 color match
Texas dandelion flower

7

PANTONE Yellow 012 color match
Yellow lucky cat bell

PANTONE®
7499 C

PANTONE 7499 color match
Ramen noodles

9

PANTONE®
108 C

10

PANTONE 108 color match
Minion Tic Tacs

PANTONE®
116 C

PANTONE®
116 C

PANTONE 116 color match
Smiley Lego head

PANTONE 116 color match
Tiny yellow Crocs sandal

PANTONE®
109 C

12

PANTONE 109 color match.
Aster flower

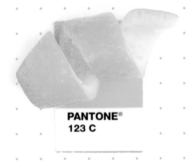

PANTONE 123 color match.
Lemon peel

13

PANTONE®
Yellow 012 C

14

PANTONE Yellow 012 color match
Yellow Skittles

PANTONE®
369 C

PANTONE®
704 C

PANTONE®
2018 C

PANTONE®
7449 C

PANTONE 369, 704, 2018, 7449 color matches
Green Skittles, red Skittles, orange Skittles,
purple Skittles

15

PANTONE®
130 C

16

PANTONE 130 color match
Mini replica of Ford Fairlane yellow taxicab

PANTONE
136 C

PANTONE 136 color match
Tiny rubber chicken

17

PANTONE®
2006 C

18

PANTONE 2006 color match
Tiny puffer fish toy

PANTONE®
7408 C

PANTONE®
7409 C

PANTONE 7408 color match
Texas coneflower

PANTONE 7409 color match
Yellow leaf from shrub

19

PANTONE®
136 C

20

PANTONE 136 color match
Inside of a kumquat

PANTONE®
7499 C

PANTONE 7499 color match
Magnolia stamens

21

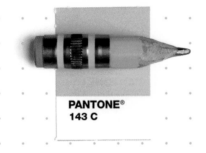

PANTONE®
143 C

22

PANTONE 143 color match
Ticonderoga #2 pencil

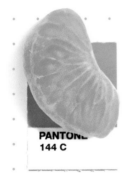

PANTONE 144 color match
Clementine segment

23

PANTONE®
2011 C

PANTONE®
7549 C

24

PANTONE 2011 color match
Goldfish cracker

PANTONE 7549 color match
Golden tickseed flower

PANTONE®
151 C

PANTONE 151 color match
Orange peel

25

PANTONE®
7577 C

PANTONE 7577 color match
Daruma doll magnet

PANTONE®
158 C

PANTONE®
466 C

PANTONE 158, 466 color matches
Little fox eraser, little bunny eraser

PANTONE®
1575 C

28

PANTONE 1575 color match
Jungle geranium flower

PANTONE®
1555 C

PANTONE®
1555 C

PANTONE 1555 color match
Underside of lucky jungle geranium flower

PANTONE 1555 color match
"Hey Babe" Valentine's Day candy

29

PANTONE®
151 C

PANTONE®
1585 C

30

PANTONE 151 color match
Lego carrot

PANTONE 1585 color match
Cheetos

CANDY-CORN ORANGE

PANTONE®
2024 C

PANTONE 2024 color match
Candy corn

31

PANTONE®
1595 C

PANTONE 1595 color match
Marigold flower

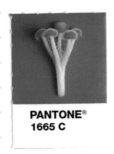

PANTONE®
1665 C

PANTONE 1665 color match
Hibiscus stigma pads

33

PANTONE®
158 C

PANTONE®
7621 C

34

PANTONE 158, 7621 color matches
Teenage Mutant Ninja Turtles: Michelangelo,
Teenage Mutant Ninja Turtles: Raphael

PANTONE®
7679 C

PANTONE®
2387 C

PANTONE 7679, 2387 color matches
Teenage Mutant Ninja Turtles: Donatello,
Teenage Mutant Ninja Turtles: Leonardo

35

PANTONE®
Orange 021 C

36   PANTONE Orange 021 color match
Deformed orange M&M's candy

PANTONE®
1655 C

PANTONE 1655 color match
Pomegranate flower bud

37

PANTONE®
7580 C

38

PANTONE 7580 color match
Tiny dragon toy

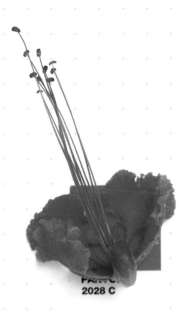

PANTONE 2028 color match
Flamboyant flower

PANTONE®
7623 C

40

PANTONE 7623 color match
Slice of tiger fig

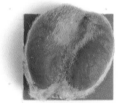

PANTONE®
7625 C

PANTONE 7625 color match
Fuzzy fruit of king sago palm

PANTONE®
7626 C

PANTONE®
200 C

PANTONE 7626 color match
Vintage bee lapel pin

PANTONE 200 color match
Glass apple pendant from Estonia

42

PANTONE®
2031 C

PANTONE®
2033 C

PANTONE 2031 color match
Red yucca flower

PANTONE 2033 color match
Bud from flowering maple

43

CHERRY-TOMATO RED

PANTONE®
7627 C

44

PANTONE 7627 color match
Inside of a cherry tomato

RADISH RED

PANTONE 1945 color match
Tiny radish

45

PANTONE®
7621 C

46

PANTONE 7621 color match
Red gumball machine charm

PANTONE®
7621 C

PANTONE 7621 color match
French cake trinket (*fève*)

47

STRAWBERRY RED

PANTONE®
7621 C

PANTONE®
201 C

48

PANTONE 7621 color match
Tiny strawberry

PANTONE 201 color match
Strawberry gummy snack

LADYBUG RED

PANTONE®
200 C

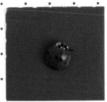

PANTONE®
484 C

PANTONE 200 color match
Glass ladybug

PANTONE 484 color match
Deceased ladybug

49

PANTONE®
1807 C

50

PANTONE 1807 color match
Red leaf from a shrub

CHERRY RED

PANTONE®
207 C

PANTONE 207 color match
Little cherry

PANTONE®
Rubine Red C

52

PANTONE Rubine Red color match
Red milkweed flower

PANTONE®
186 C

PANTONE 186 color match
Begonia flower

54

PANTONE 220 color match
Drummond phlox flower

PANTONE®
704 C

PANTONE®
7427 C
⅋

PANTONE 704 color match
Half-opened red bottlebrush flower

PANTONE 7427 color match
Magnolia seeds

55

PANTONE®
7421 C

PANTONE®
7421 C

PANTONE 7421 color match
Crepe myrtle seed head

PANTONE 7421 color match
Anasazi beans

56

PANTONE®
7421 C

PANTONE 7421 color match
Japanese maple seedpod

PANTONE®
1915 C
⊛

PANTONE®
258 C
⊛

58

PANTONE 1915, 258 color matches
Pink dinosaur sprinkles, purple dinosaur sprinkles

PANTONE®
382 C

PANTONE 382 color match
Lime dinosaur sprinkles

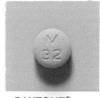

PANTONE®
189 C

PANTONE®
212 C

PANTONE 189 color match
Blood pressure control tablet

PANTONE 212 color match
Pink gem biscuit

60

PANTONE® 2030 C

PANTONE® 210 C

PANTONE 2030 color match
Daruma doll magnet

PANTONE 210 color match
Butterfly Fairy Barbie shoe

PANTONE®
7635 C

62

PANTONE 7635 color match
Cupcake ring charm

PANTONE®
7423 C

PANTONE®
5605 C

PANTONE 7423 color match
Pink polka dot plant leaf

PANTONE 5605 color match
Pink polka dot plant leaf with reversed colors

63

PANTONE
2352 C

64   PANTONE 2352 color match
          Half-opened Texas sage flower

PANTONE®
2352 C

PANTONE 2352 color match
Tolumnia Genting "Pink Lady" orchid

65

PANTONE®
237 C

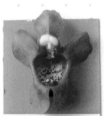

PANTONE®
244 C

66

PANTONE 237 color match
Touch-me-not flower

PANTONE 244 color match
Orchid-like tiny pink flower

PANTONE 2351 color match
Redbud flowers

67

PANTONE®
496 C

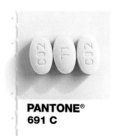

PANTONE®
691 C

PANTONE 496 color match
Indian hawthorn flower

PANTONE 691 color match
Simvastatin tablets

PANTONE®
706 C

PANTONE 706 color match
Pink cotton candy

PANTONE®
2100 C

70

PANTONE 2100 color match
Purple mushroom eraser

PANTONE®
7676 C

PANTONE 7676 color match
Mini hair clip

LAVENDER

PANTONE®
667 C

PANTONE 667 color match
Lavender

PANTONE®
2725 C

⚘

PANTONE®
519 C

PANTONE 2725 color match
Bluebonnet flower

PANTONE 519 color match
Alligator flag flower

73

PANTONE®
5145 C

PANTONE®
114 C

PANTONE®
178 C

PANTONE®
359 C

74

PANTONE 5145, 114, 178, 359 color matches
Purple Froot Loops, yellow Froot Loops,
pink Froot Loops, green Froot Loops

PANTONE® 7671 C

PANTONE 7671 color match
Tiny purple dragon toy

PANTONE®
7658 C

76

PANTONE 7658 color match
Ornamental cabbage leaf

PANTONE
7678 C

PANTONE®
7679 C

PANTONE 7678 color match
Fairy fan flower

PANTONE 7679 color match
Victoria blue salvia flower

PANTONE®
5115 C

78

PANTONE 5115 color match
Thai basil flowers

PANTONE®
2355 C

PANTONE 2355 color match
Beautyberries

PANTONE®
Purple C

80

PANTONE Purple color match
Prairie larkspur flowers

PANTONE®
2645 C

PANTONE 2645 color match
Fall aster flower

PANTONE®
2716 C

82

PANTONE 2716 color match
Blue plumbago flower

PANTONE 649 color match
Flax lilies

83

PANTONE®
537 C

PANTONE 537 color match
Cameo charm

PANTONE®
7683 C

PANTONE 7683 color match
Stamp from the United Kingdom

PANTONE®
2172 C

PANTONE 2172 color match
Blue owl bell

PANTONE®
2935 C

PANTONE 2935 color match
Lego Steve from Minecraft

88

PANTONE Blue 072 color match
Union Jack Popobe pluggy

PANTONE 2735 color match
Souvenir Eiffel Tower thimble

BLUEBERRY

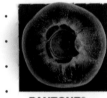

PANTONE®
433 C

PANTONE 433 color match
Blueberry

PANTONE®
540 C

PANTONE 540 color match
Rattla Lego head

PANTONE®
7667 C

PANTONE 7667 color match
Blue plaid coquina shell

PANTONE®
621 C

PANTONE 621 color match
Half shell of a robin's egg

93

PANTONE®
5565 C

94

PANTONE 5565 color match
Jade pendant

PANTONE®
7472 C

PANTONE 7472 color match
Turquoise earring

95

PANTONE®
628 C

96

PANTONE 628 color match
Blue cotton candy

PANTONE 7475 color match
Mini Statue of Liberty

97

PANTONE®
2235 C

98

PANTONE 2235 color match
Poison dart frog toy

PANTONE®
362 C

PANTONE 362 color match
Tiny T. rex

PANTONE®
575 C

PANTONE®
575 C

100

PANTONE 575 color match
Baby acorn

PANTONE 575 color match
Young red yucca seedpod

PANTONE®
7496 C

PANTONE 7496 color match
Young seedpod of Indian shot flower

101

PANTONE®
5625 C

102

PANTONE 5625 color match
Burro's tail succulent

PANTONE®
5635 C

PANTONE 5635 color match
Succulent rosette

PANTONE®
2300 C

104

PANTONE 2300 color match
Edamame bean

PANTONE®
364 C

PANTONE 364 color match
Peas-in-a-pod bracelet charm

AS GREEN AS GRASS

PANTONE
575 C

106

PANTONE 575 color match
Grass

CLOVER GREEN

PANTONE®
2279 C

PANTONE 2279 color match
Clover leaf

PANTONE®
363 C

PANTONE 363 color match
1940s celluloid horse gumball charm

PANTONE®
559 C

PANTONE 559 color match
Tiny sleeping mouse Christmas ornament

PANTONE®
5645 C

110

PANTONE 5645 color match
Underside of fuzzy Texas sage leaf

IVY

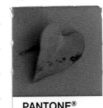

PANTONE®
7491 C

PANTONE 7491 color match
Baby ivy leaf

PANTONE®
5773 C

112

PANTONE 5773 color match
Witch's hair lichen

PANTONE®
7495 C

PANTONE®
5777 C

PANTONE 7495 color match
Young magnolia seedpod

PANTONE 5777 color match
Green seed puff of firewheel flower

PANTONE®
5767 C

PANTONE®
371 C

PANTONE 5767 color match
Young bald cypress cone

PANTONE 371 color match
Water lily seedpod

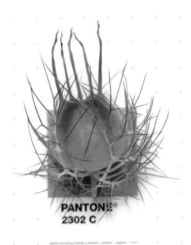

PANTONE 2302 color match
Love-in-a-mist seedpod

GREEN APPLE

PANTONE®
2305 C

PANTONE 2305 color match
Young green apple with a heart-shaped mark

PANTONE®
2280 C

PANTONE®
7495 C

PANTONE 2280 color match
Young fruit from foxtail fern

PANTONE 7495 color match
Rose hip

PANTONE®
2255 C

118

PANTONE 2255 color match
Lucky Charms green marshmallow hat

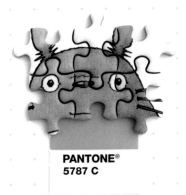

PANTONE®
5787 C

PANTONE 5787 color match
Pieces from Totoro mini puzzle

PANTONE®
2276 C

120

PANTONE 2276 color match
Brussels sprout

PANTONE®
383 C

PANTONE 383 color match
Lime peel

PANTONE®
371 C

122

PANTONE 371 color match
Bluebonnet seedpod

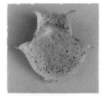

PANTONE®
2404 C

PANTONE 2404 color match
Young Atlantic white cedar cone

PANTONE®
450 C

PANTONE®
5815 C

124

PANTONE 450 color match
Crepe myrtle seedpod

PANTONE 5815 color match
Crepe myrtle fruit

ACORN BROWN

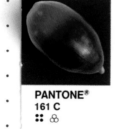

PANTONE®
161 C

PANTONE 161 color match
Acorn

PANTONE®
2318 C

126

PANTONE 2318 color match
Squirrel miniature garden decoration

PANTONE®
7508 C

PANTONE 7508 color match
Pecan

128

PANTONE 872 color match
Brass rabbit head charm

PANTONE®
874 C

PANTONE 874 color match
Brass bee charm

PANTONE®
482 C

130

PANTONE 482 color match
Seashell from Galveston Beach

PANTONE 2312 color match
Coconut shell button

PANTONE 7502 color match
Buna-shimeji mushroom

131

PANTONE®
4505 C

PANTONE®
Black 5 C

132

PANTONE 4505 color match
Cardamom pods

PANTONE Black 5 color match
Cloves

PANTONE® 4635 C

PANTONE 4635 color match
Star anise seedpod

PANTONE®
Cool Gray 8 C

134

PANTONE Cool Gray 8 color match
Lego ray gun

PANTONE®
423 C

PANTONE®
877 C

PANTONE 423 color match
Tiny plastic elephant

PANTONE 877 color match
Wedding ring

135

PANTONE®
7503 C

136

PANTONE 7503 color match
Lentils

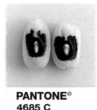

PANTONE®
4685 C

PANTONE®
Black 4 C

PANTONE 4685 color match
Black-eyed peas

PANTONE Black 4 color match
Starbucks Sumatra dark roast coffee bean

137

PANTONE®
407 C

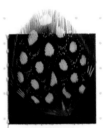

PANTONE®
Black 2 C

138

PANTONE 407 color match
Unidentified bird feather

PANTONE Black 2 color match
Guinea fowl feather

BLACKBERRY

PANTONE®
518 C

PANTONE 518 color match
Blackberry

PANTONE®
439 C

140

PANTONE 439 color match
Mini Oreo cookie

MILK-CHOCOLATE BROWN

PANTONE®
7568 C

PANTONE 7568 color match
Cadbury chocolate

PANTONE®
468 C

PANTONE 468 color match
1940s celluloid chicken gumball charm

ACKNOWLEDGMENTS

I'm dedicating this fun book to:

My dear husband, Sunil, and my two kids, Aron and Nora. Thank you for filling up my life with colors and wonderful things, the kind that cannot be captured on little PANTONE color chips.

My followers on Tumblr and Instagram, without whom this book would not have happened. Thank you for sharing my love of colors and cute tiny things.

Pantone, for creating such wonderful color-matching systems. And ABRAMS, for giving me the wonderful opportunity to have my "Tiny PMS Match" project produced as a book.

My God, who created the small bright-blue flower that grew in my front yard, from which the "Tiny PMS Match" project came to be.

Editor: Samantha Weiner
Designer: Darilyn Lowe Carnes
Production Manager: True Sims

Library of Congress Control Number: 2015955481

ISBN: 978-1-4197-2087-1

Printed and bound in the United States
10 9 8 7 6 5 4 3 2 1

Abrams Image books are available at special discounts when purchased in quantity for
premiums and promotions as well as fundraising or educational use. Special editions can
also be created to specification. For details, contact specialsales@abramsbooks.com or
the address below.

THE ART OF BOOKS SINCE 1949
115 West 18th Street
New York, NY 10011
www.abramsbooks.com